UNCOMMON,
CLEAN, COUNTRY BOY JOKES

GRANGER RAY MARTIN, SR.

Copyright © 2021
2nd edition Printing
Mt. Olive, NC | GCS PUBLISHING

ISBN: 978-1-970179-00-2
All rights reserved.
No part of this publication may be reproduced, distributed, or transmitted in any form or by any means, including photocopying, recording, or other electronic or mechanical methods, without the prior written permission of the publisher, except in the case of brief quotations embodied in critical reviews and certain other noncommercial uses permitted by copyright law.

Editors: Tiara Martin Brown & Ronald Chunn
Cover & Layout Design: Start Write Publish | Rainah Martin Davis
Illustrations: Lawrence Dwight Durham
Executive Producers: Tara Martin Crews & Tiara Martin Brown
Ruby Martin Simmons & Rainah Martin Davis

PREFACE

Peter Rabbit Eat a Fish, Alligator Catch an Eel

The above saying was gleaned from my mom over sixty years ago. It was how to spell a preface. This joke book and funny stories is dedicated to my mom, Pennie Marie Ward Martin who often kept us in stitches. She loved to tell the story of the blind man passing the fish market. He tips his hat and says "Good evening ladies!" Apparently, the smell was so overwhelming he thought he had encountered a group of women menstruating!

Another favorite of hers was the talking mule. Man claims he has a talking mule. Goes to the mule's rear end and asked "Mule, do you want some oats?" The mule raises his tail and goes "a fewwwww aaaah!" For those of you who have never heard a mule pass gas, this is the sound the mule makes.

Some of the punch lines may be a bit corny. My daughters would often tell me, "Dad, never quit your day job!" This may happen after a particular corny joke.

I dedicate this book to all my children and grandchildren. May this book add quality to your life and life to your quality! And may your good always be your better, and your better your very best. When you lay me to rest, pick out your favorite and pass the test (torch!)

Table of Contents

Just Country	7
Senior Citizens	17
Motivation	21
Enthusiasm	41
Real Life Stories	45
My Family	51
In the Bible	57
Stay in the Church	59
One Liners with a Point	63
Whatever and Risqué	69
Singing	75
Epilogue	82

Chapter One

JUST COUNTRY

Break Them from Sucking Eggs

Your dog is constantly eating the chicken eggs. To break him/her from sucking the eggs or anyone from doing something that you don't want, the farmer uses this trick:

He injects about six eggs with cayenne pepper and leaves them for the dog who eagerly begins to suck on each egg. The eggs are hot going down but even hotter when they come out the other end. This will "break them from sucking eggs."

I often use as a metaphor when I want to get someone to change what they are doing.

How to Catch a Chicken Snake.

For you city folks who have never encountered a chicken snake that goes into your hen house and swallows the eggs whole, this is a workable trick that I learned from Amway Diamond, Kay Fletcher, a number of years ago:

Drill a one inch hole near the ground outside and place an egg there. Then place another egg on the inside. The snake swallows the first egg, looks thru the hole, sees the second egg and swallows that one too. Now the snake is caught between the devil and the deep blue sea. Take a shovel cut the snake in half and you get both eggs back (I wouldn't eat them)!

Saran Wrap

My rap is so tight, it's like Saran Wrap.

My rap is so strong, it's like Reynolds aluminum fold.

My rap is so good, it's like Goodness gracious!

Conversation Between Two North Carolina Duck Hunters

M R   DUCKS
M R   Not
O S A R
C M   Wangs
L I B
M R   Ducks

Translation for New Yorkers:

Them are Ducks.
Them are Not.
Oh Yes They Are
See them Wings
Hell I be!
Them are Ducks (You can also use with Birds)

Hush Puppies

There are different stories about the origin of hush puppies. As the slaves from the big house tried to take food to their relatives in the field the dogs would bark. In order to keep them quiet and not give them the good food, the cooks would fry pieces of meal, toss them to the dogs and say "hush puppies, hush!"

They eventually became a tasty staple for use in the south with chopped bbq, which was my favorite growing up. I also love them with fish dinner.

Now That Takes the Cake!

On Saturday nights the slaves would gather in the barn for a cake baking contest and general fun!

Each person would put on the Master's shoes or the Mistresses shoes and strut their stuff. Whoever did the best at the strutting would get the whole cake, "Now that takes the Cake!"

Total Commitment

Mr. Pig and Ms. Chicken were walking along the road and they spotted a billboard. Ms. Chicken loudly exclaimed to Mr. Pig that together they were the great American breakfast "ham and eggs".

Mr. Pig with a bit of sophisticated sarcasm says, "For you it's just a days work, but for me it is total commitment".

My First Job

This is not my first job.
I have done so much,
For so many,
For so little,
That I am now qualified
To do almost anything
For anybody,
At any price!

My Very First Job

I started out on the farm as a young lad.
We worked from can't see in the morning,
To can't see at night.

The earliest job I had was a pilot.
I would see manure in the stall.
My job was to "pile it" on the outside!
Now, I want to be a jet pilot,
So that I can "pile it" at the speed of sound!

Milking Cows

Cows Don't Give Milk...So you thought that cows give milk? As a farm boy having to milk cows twice a day, I can say with certified proof that you "Have to take every drop!"

Pig with Peg Leg
(contributed by Luby Martin)

A traveling salesman passes a house and sees a pig leaning against the house with shades on, smoking a pipe, and drinking a can of beer.

Totally overcome with curiosity, he turns around, drives back to the house, gets out his car, and knocks on the farmer's door.

He describes his fascinations about the pig, wearing shades, smoking a pipe and leaning against the house. He now notices that the pig has a wooden leg.

The farmer explains that this is a very special pig. One night while he and the wife were at prayer meeting, this pig saved the lives of all three of his kids when the house caught on fire. Now that this special pig gets to eat what he wants, drinks what he wants and smokes a pipe.

So the salesman, now curious about the peg wooden leg says "tell me about the wooden leg, did he lose it in the fire"? "Oh No!" says the farmer. "This is a special pig and we just couldn't eat it all in one setting. We are saving the best parts for Thanksgiving and Christmas!"

Hooray for Our Side!

Lady Godiva rode side saddle without any panties. The shout would go up, "Hooray for our side!" As she passed by, they tried to get the right angle so they could shout "Hooray for our side" with maximum enthusiasm.

Don't Let Them Get Your Goat!

There is a common expression in the south: the origin of which comes from horse racing. If your horse was excited during the night for whatever the reason, the horse would not perform the next day.

To keep the horse calm, the horse would be paired with a goat. Goats are very stubborn and very hard to upset. If the competitor wanted to mess your horse up for the next day, they would often steal the goat and win the race! In other words, keep your goat locked and safe and don't let anyone get next to you.

Three Types of People

There are three types of people in the world:

Those that can count and those that cannot. Obviously, I am one that cannot count.

Farmer Finds a Rope

My father as a farmer was often and daily OUT-standing in his field!

One day a farmer (my dad in his later years) was standing in the middle of the field. Momentarily lost in thought, he couldn't remember whether he had lost a cow or found a rope! It is amazing how the mind can go so fast!

Three-Legged Chicken

A traveling salesman was going south on I-95 just outside of Jacksonville, Florida driving 70 mph when he was passed by a three-legged chicken.

Out of curiosity, when the chicken turned down a dirt path, he followed the chicken to a farmhouse. The chicken then went into an enclosed area where more three-legged chickens were housed.

He knocked on the door of the farmhouse and the proprietor came out. He inquired about the three-legged chicken. The farmer replied that yup, that is a three-legged chicken that he genetically engineered.

The salesman wanted to know why? He said that his family loved chickens. He liked the legs, his wife liked the legs, and when Bubba Jr. came along he liked the legs too. So to appease everyone, he engineered the three legs.

"Wow!," said the salesman! "How do they taste?" The farmer then shrugged his shoulders and with high pitch in his voice said, "We don't know. We've never been able to catch, clean, and consume one!"

Chapter Two

SENIOR CITIZENS

A man is as young as the woman he feels!
Now that I am 71,

I know how to feel younger!

Why Marry a Senior Citizen!

They don't yell,
They don't tell,
They don't smell,
And when you sock it to them,
They're grateful as hell! (Moms Mabely)

True story: I was selling subscriptions for the Goldsboro News Argus at a Food Lion in Goldsboro. This elderly lady stopped at my booth, ordered a paper and proceeded to tell me why the best choice for me would be a cougar (old white women, but I prefer Jaguar, for Black or Brown women).

She says that young women don't know their rear end from a hole in the ground. They will waste all your money trying to look cute, but cute don't buy happiness and beauty just fades away. She also explained that since such a woman would have passed the child bearing stage, she could devote all her attention to her husband. An elderly woman has wisdom beyond her age and if she is godly you get double for your trouble.

Because she had spent money with me on a subscription, I listened and married Peggy Jean Patterson and I truly married above my pay grade!

Old Age

Three Signs of Old Age...First the Memory goes... Dang, I forgot the other two!

And don't tell anyone it's eyesight and hearing. You might embarrass them!

Three Sisters Ages 72, 73, and 74

The sista that was 74 said to the sista that was 72, "I think I will go upstairs and take a bath." At the foot of the stairs, she turned to her sista who was 72 and asked, "Was I going upstairs or coming downstairs? " About that time the 73 year old with one foot in the tub and the other one out, shouted downstairs to the 72 year old, "Was I getting in the tub or getting out of the tub?"

The 72 year old then exclaimed very sarcastically, "Heaven help us, I am glad I'm not like either of you, knock on wood!" Then she turns her head to the front door and says, "I'll be there in a minute! I think someone is at the front door!"

Senior Citizens Remember

If you're White, then alright! (White Privilege!)
If you're Black, get back! (Back of the Bus!)
If you're Brown, stick around! (Every Field Worker!)
If you're Yellow, stay mellow! (The Other Fellow!)
If you're near White, green Light!

BLACK LIVES MATTER!

Chapter Three

MOTIVATION

Break is Over... Back On Your Heads!

Lucifer is introducing a new candidate to the afterlife. The candidate looks in one room and they are standing in manure up to their chins.

In the second room the manure is up to their waists.

In the third room, they are drinking coffee and the manure is only ankle deep. The candidate, with a smirk on his face says, "I'll take this one to spend eternity in." As he enters the room, a whistle blows and the loud speaker loudly explains. "OK, the break is over, back standing on your heads!"

Dog on the Porch

An old hound dog was sitting on the porch of an old farm house. Occasionally, he would raise his head and howl. A visitor wanted to know why. The owner replied, "He's sitting on a briar." The visitor replied, "Why doesn't he get up and remove the briar?" The owner replied, "Well, it's like this, it hurts enough to complain about but not enough that he would try to do something about it!"

Define Work

Youngsters today don't have any concept of work. I worked on a farm. We usually worked from can't see in the morning to can't see at night! Here's my "best definition of work."

It's about 10pm and you are in the racks of the tobacco barn. You are on the bottom rack. Your brother is about four racks higher than you. Because of the extreme heat, you both are stripped to the waist. You poke up a stick of tied tobacco and as you bend down to grab the next stick coming to you, a drop of liquid hits your back.

For a moment, you are frozen in time! Is that dew water from the tobacco that you primed at 6:30am (cold)? Or is that perspiration from my brother above (98.6

degrees of perspiration)? As the mixture settles into the perspiration on your body, you realize that it is cold and refreshing. You smile, poke that stick of tobacco up and praise God you are alive and doing quite well in North Carolina in mid-July.

Cross-eyed Disc Thrower

I am your motivational speaker for this occasion. I usually don't set any records while I perform. I am sorta like a cross-eyed disc thrower. I generally keep the crowd alert as I perform. (They never know where I'm gonna throw the disc!)

I won't Keep You Long

My response to audience members that wonder "How long is this gonna take?" is this:

I say, "I'm gonna tell you what Marilyn Monore told her fifth husband, "I am not gonna keep you too long!""

Money

My money is funny,
My change is strange,
My nickel is fickle,
My dime, not on time,
My quarter won't hold water,
My fifty cents, don't make sense,
My dollar bill don't have no thrill!
Fact is my money is hilarious,
Just like you for asking me for "mo" money!
Go get yourself a job!

Story: Seven Cow Wife

According to a certain fable, there once was a villager that had a daughter that didn't quite fill the bill. To put it mildly, an average daughter was worth between five to seven cows as a dowry. In the father's mind he could expect around three but no more.

On a certain day, in a certain month, a traveler to the village approached the father and wanted to pay the dowry for this young lady. We don't know what it was but something about this damsel really fascinated this traveler.

The traveler knew that he would have to pay the maximum for his bride to be. The father, on the other hand only asked for three cows. The traveler, shocked, insisted that he pay the maximum for his bride to be. After several hours of hassling, the father finally accepted the dowry of seven cows and the traveler left with his prize.

Several years passed and the traveler returned with the most beautiful lady in the world. The father was stunned and wanted to know what happened to his daughter! The traveler replied that within her, he knew he had a seven cow wife and everyday instead of focusing on her outside, he would remind her that she was truly a "seven cow wife!" Beauty is only skin deep but words can cut or they can heal!

The Sorry Horse "Tail"

Apparently this fellow had a sorry horse that he wanted to sell. Every day at that bar, after a few rounds he would tell everyone just how sorry the horse is. Finally one day, someone pulled the gentleman aside and told him that unless he started to brag on his horse that no one would buy that horse.

So he wised up and started to praise the horse. He would say, "I've got the smartest horse. He could do everything but talk. He could count, he could feed himself, he could exercise totally on his own. One day a stranger (who had never heard the real story) approached the owner and offered him a tidy sum. The owner refused and countered with double the price and more flattery about the horse.

They then shook hands and the deal was set. After that, the original owner never showed up again. But the new owner showed up and started to bad mouth the sorry horse until the guy that had counseled the original owner schooled him. About this time the original owner started to show his face again and the new owner bragged about the horse until the original owner wanted to buy the horse back!

The moral of the story is always brag about your horse or you will be stuck with a sorry horse! I have to outrun you!

What is a Friend for?

Two close friends were out on a mountain trail when suddenly they spot a bear. One hiker, sits down, and slips on his running shoes. While the other one looks at him in absolute amazement and says "Hey bro, you can't out run that bear!" He chuckled, "I don't have to outrun the bear, I just have to outrun you!"

The Turtle and The Scorpion... Nature

In middle Africa during the rainy season, a scorpion comes upon a rushing river that was usually a dry bed. He mused about how to get across. About that time a turtle approached and he decided to hitch a ride.

The scorpion and turtle are natural enemies and never get along. The scorpion asked for a ride across the river. The reaction of the turtle was classic, "NO! In the middle of the river you will sting me in the neck and we will both die!"

The scorpion (Evil Convivial) continued to persist in his arguments until finally it was getting late and he wanted to make it to the other side before sunset.

When they get to the middle of the raging river, suddenly the scorpion is overcome with evil passion and stings the turtle in the neck. With his last breath, the turtle ask, "WHY, WHY, WHY? Now we both die!" The scorpion shrugs his shoulders and replies, "It is in my nature and you knew this could happen."

Things Not Always as They Seem

A bird was flying in the middle of winter and flew just a little too high. Because his wings were wet, the frigid temperature froze his wings and he tumbled to the ground in the middle of a cow pasture.

While he laid there nearly froze to death, a cow came by and dumped manure all over his body. The heat from the manure, melted the ice on his wings. Very excited, he started to sing.

A big yellow mellow cat, heard the singing, dug him out and ate him for dinner!

Three morals of this story:

One, everyone who sh!ts on you is not your enemy.

Two, anyone who digs you out of sh!t is not necessarily your friend.

Three, when you are up to your eyeballs in sh!t, don't sing, just pray!

Two Men

Two men look out
the prison bars!
One saw mud,
the other saw stars!

The glass is always
Half full for the optimist
And half empty for the pessimist.
Always stay positive!

Magna Cum Laude..

I graduated with honors...Magna Cum Laude. Most of my friends, however, graduated with praise..."Thank you Lordy".

Hunting License

Two hunters were out in the woods when they spotted the game warden. One hunter, throws down his bag limit, runs through the woods, down the hill, crosses a stream and just before climbing a fence, the warden catches him.

The game warden requests to see his license. He very carefully pulls out his wallet, removes every piece of paper, and finally presents his license.

After the warden examines a perfectly valid license, the warden says, "This license is valid and up to date. Why did you run?" He replied, "My friend Harry did not have a license! I gave him time to get away". (Nature of true friendship.)

Cat That Sat on a Hot Stove

Experience is a good teacher. Believe it or not, a cat that has set on a hot stove will never sit on another stove hot or cold!

Two Bulls on the Hill

An old bull and a young bull are on a hill top. They look down in the valley and see a whole bunch of heifers.

Young bull: Hey, let's run down the hill and make love to one of those heifers.

Old bull: No, no, no, young fella. Let's WALK down the hill and make love to ALL them fine heifers!

Two Bulls in the Pen

Two really sorry bulls on a farm were not getting the job done. So the farmer went and brought a real bull. On the way home, the sorry bulls could hear the new bull just bellowing and snorting.

Suddenly, one of the bulls starts to paw the earth and throw up grass. The other bull says, "What is your problem, why are you behaving like that?" The bull says, "I want that new fellow to know that I am a bull too!"

Story: It is Not Your Baby

In a village far away, the native women on wash day were at the rivers' edge washing their clothes when a great bald eagle flies down and snatches up her young baby.

The natives quickly jump into action. They ran and got the best climbers in the village but they could not get to the eagle's nest on the steep, unclimbable side of the mountain and gave up in total shame and humiliation.

Suddenly someone shouts, "Look!" And they see the mother with her shawl, beat back the eagle, take her shawl, cradle the baby in it and descend the mountain.

The villagers rush over in total disbelief and want to know how she made the climb and rescued her baby! "How did you do it when the best climbers in the village were not able to do it?" Her answer, "It was not your baby!"

Would You Like to Buy a Toothbrush?

Three salesmen went out to sell toothbrushes. One sold ten, one sold twenty. The winner for that day sold 100 toothbrushes.

When quizzed on his technique, he stated that he had gone to the airport, and offered people pate'. They responded, "This tastes like mud!" He replied, "It is! Wanna buy a toothbrush?"

Would... You... Like... For... Me...to... Read...it ...to...You?

Two Bible salesmen report their efforts. The greatest salesman had sold ten Bibles. However, the inexperienced neophyte, on his first day, had sold fifty. No one could beat it! Especially since he had a stuttering problem. His explanation shocked everyone.

He greeted everyone with the opening line that got a closing 100% of the time. He had offered to read the Bible to them!

Things You Cannot Do!

You cannot put toothpaste back in a tube.
You cannot climb a fence leaning toward you,
And you cannot kiss a girl leaning away from you!

The Higher the Level, The Bigger the Devil

In the religious world you have to remember that the lay person deals with little devils, the leaders deal with medium sized devils, the pastor deals with large devils, but the Bishop has to deal with great big evil. However, there is no power of the devil greater than Jehovah, Yahweh. Yahhavah is ALL Powerful and your words must grow stronger!

The Pipe Fitter

I'm not the Pipe Fitter,
Nor the Pipe Fitter's son.
But I'll fit the pipe,
Until the pipe fitter cums!

Stutter Shutter

Go my son and shut the shutter,
This I heard my mother utter.
Shutter is shut,
The boy did mutter!
I can't shut her any further!

The Roughed Rock

Around the rough and rugged rock,
The ragged rascal ran!

Seashells

She sells seashells by the sea shore!

Lead a Horse to Water

You have often heard it said that you can lead a horse to water but you can't make them drink.

My good friend Diamond Direct, Dewey Tobias added that you must salt the oats. In other words, find their motivation. Everyone has a hot button, a purpose, a motivation. Sell the sizzle not the steak!

Definition of Expert:

Technically, if you are fifty miles from home, in another city, another state, or another country you can be considered an expert.

An ex-husband, ex-wife, ex-boyfriend, or ex-girl is a thing of the past. Spurt is a drip of water under pressure. An expert is someone who has been under pressure!

Always Work in Pairs

One can put a thousand to flight.
Two can put ten thousand to flight,
However, a Triple braided cord is not easily broken!
Together Everyone Achieves More…T.E.A.M.

False Evidence Appearing Real........F.E.A.R.
The only place where money comes before WORK, is in the dictionary.

Documentation Beats Conversation

This is just one of those phrases that sticks with you. In the middle of any heated debate about the facts, always have your documentation. Whether in court, at work, in a family dispute or even in church! Documentation beats conversation! Let the evidence do the talking. It speaks so loudly that I can't hear a word you are saying!

Destructive Motivation

I saw them tearing a building down,
A gang of men in my hometown.
With a heave and a ho,
Then yes, yes, yell!
They swung a ball
And the whole wall fell!

So, I said to the foreman,
"Are these the skills,
You would use
If you had to build?"

"Oh, no! The most common labor,
is all I need!
I can destroy in one day
What it takes skilled men,
Ten years to build!"

Patient vulture in a tree: Patience my ass, I'm gonna kill something!

Repetition

As a motivational speaker was leaving the stage he heard someone say that his presentation was lousy. A bit shocked, the host quickly added, "Don't pay any attention to him, he's just repeating what he heard someone else say!"

Some People

There are some people
That take all they can.
Bake all they take.
Can all they can.
Then sit on their cans!

Sign in a Mechanics Shop: 301 Service Center, Dunn, NC Peter Chance, Owner

We do three types of jobs here: Cheap, Fast, Good. Choose any two.

If you want it Cheap and Fast, it will not be Good.

If you want it Cheap and Good, it will not be Fast.

If you want it Good and Fast, it will not be Cheap.

Choose carefully and we both will be happy!

Chapter Four

ENTHUSIASM

Ten Inch Pianist

A young man sits down at an empty bar stool in the local pub. The gentleman next to him strikes up a conversation. Then he reaches inside his coat pocket, pulls out a miniature piano, a small stool, then a pianist who begins to play beautifully.

The young man was amazed and wanted to know where he could get such an arrangement. The gentleman then reaches in another pocket and pulls out an oriental looking lamp. He retorts, rubs this lamp and makes a wish.

He rubs the lamp and requests a million bucks. Suddenly, there is the sound of a rushing mighty wind and in the door flies one million ducks! The young man loudly exclaims, "I wished for a million bucks, not a million ducks!"

The gentleman explains, "I understand, my request was for a ten inch penis, not a ten inch pianist!"

Enthusiasm: Chickens vs Ducks

There is one good reason we eat lots of chicken eggs but very seldom ducks eggs! Apparently the reason is enthusiasm. When a duck lays an egg it proclaims "Whack", then walks away.

However, when a chicken lays her prize possession she goes "Cluck, cluck, cluck..." because she wants the world to know that she is a producer!

Words alone may often fail, so demonstrate to make the sale! And make sure to use lots of enthusiasm.

You are Passionate

A lady who was three sheets into the wind, needed a ride home. A young aspiring handsome guy volunteered to take her home. When he got near the address, the inebriated lady looks at him and says "You're passionate!"

He responded his thanks, and continued to drive. She repeats herself with just a bit more enthusiasm. "You're passionate!" Again he thanks her and says to the lady, "I thought you lived around here!?" She raises her voice, looks him directly in the face and says "I told you before... YOU ARE PASSING IT!"

So Good...

If you eat something really delicious... I often say "If you put some on your forehead, your tongue will slap your brains out!" (Judge Ziglar on Amway Queen Cookware).

Chapter Five

REAL LIFE STORIES

True Story: My daughter never laughed at my jokes until she was admitted.

My daughter, T.C. was Baker Acted due to an episode she was having. Highly intelligent, built like a model, and a beautiful, athletic volleyball player standing 6'1', she just got caught up trying to do too much!

When I went to visit her, she said that some girl kept following her around the hospital saying, "I love pu$$y, I love pu$$y, I love pu$$y!" So finally, she turned to her in a loud voice full of confidence and said, "I love d!ck!" I laughed so hard I nearly peed on myself.

Mr. Empire (My Bobble Head) is a Colored Man

I used to sell flooring for Empire Today, a major flooring company. On one occasion I ended up in a home that had probably never had a black man in it before. I gave them a bobble head from the company and told them that the one in my car is colored! I then said I colored it!

They were not amused. The wife then says to me, "I am a sheriff, my husband is a judge. If you treat us the least bit wrong, I will lock you up and my husband will throw away the key. Within 15 minutes I was out of there and calling that a bad memory!"

Resume: I Have Done So Much...

On one of my last job teaching appointments, my principal says to me that I should apply as a Special Education teacher based upon my experiences. I replied that, "I have done so much, for so many, for so little, that I now qualify to do almost anything for anybody at any price!"

Which was taken from:

> We the unwilling,
> Working for the unknowing,
> During the impossible,
> For the ungrateful,
> Have done so much
> For so long,
> For so many.
> That we are now qualified
> To do anything
> For anybody
> At any price!

> Author Unknown

How Are You?

Sermon on Blessings

I am blessed by the best,
Too blessed to be stressed.
Too anointed to be disappointed.
Too equipped to be whipped,
Too fine to be wine,
Of any kind at any time!

And now that I know the Sabbath Rest,
I can pass the Mark of the Beast Test.
Preaching from the Three Angels crest.
I can pass the test
Because I know more than the rest.
And I'm better than the best!

Good better best,
Never let it rest.
Until your good is better,
Your better is your best
And the best (Heaven)
IS YET TO COME!

Husband: The Steering Wheel Did Not Move

A darling couple, dressed to impress with matching outfits are tooling down the road. They reflect on the romantic days of the past. The husband is comfortable behind the wheel while the wife hugs the passenger door with great enthusiasm.

The wife reflects on the time when they were so close that it was difficult to tell if their was one or two people in the car. She then lets out a sigh and says to the husband that they are not romantic like they used to be.

The husband, with a bit of disdain looks squarely at the wife and says, "Well honey, I am still in the same position, behind the wheel, guess who moved?"

Chapter Six

MY FAMILY

Short Stories

My Brother Luby is 49% right, and just like my mom, thinks that he is always right. Once he thought he was mistaken, but he was wrong!

We always had plenty to eat when we were growing up. If I ever asked for seconds, I was told that I had had plenty! Go figure.

Never go for the last biscuit with a bare hand, was a standard at the breakfast table because someone else always had a fork... this was a great way to lose a hand!

Brother Billy always wanted just one biscuit when the call went out for that last biscuit. I don't know how many he actually had eaten before that. All I know is that I had eaten at least a half dozen.

ME: I Have 4 Children... All Boyz except three girls named Tia, Tara and Tiara!

My Spouse and my jokes were always a misfit until I met Peggy J. Patterson. She thinks all my jokes are hilarious and always just laughs when I have something to say! A lesson learned from the school of hard knocks!

Brother Fred and Special Ed (age 16, 58 yrs, 3 Glorias) is a classic for me. Fred ended up owning his own cooking entity and had a car washing enterprise. After many years at the Mount Olive Pickle Plant, he had amazed quite a retirement.

My Momma was feared and respected by all. Black men revered her, white men feared her, and no woman could alive could touch the hem of her garment. You had to come to her right or not come at all!

If it "Don't make dollars it doesn't make sense!"...was the favorite phrase of the now deceased and Regional Vice President of Primerica, George Kenneth Martin, my older brother and mentor.

Poppa was not a rolling stone...1696 was where he made home. When he left us, we were more than just alone!

Black Soldiers "Getting Down" Under Fire!

This is another tale by my mother. She stated that the main reason so many blacks were killed in Vietnam is that when they were told to "Git Down", they got up and started to dance!

My Baby Girl Tiara

Tara, Tiara, and I were traveling from Florida to Mount Olive, NC. About halfway, I got sleepy and asked Tara, age 12, to tap my face to wake me up. She politely refused.

About fifteen minutes later, Tiara, age 4, who had been watching me nod in the rear view mirror said, "Tara watch this!" The girl hit me so hard that I literally saw stars.

At the time, I was in the hammer (passing lane). I then moved to the granny lane, pulled off the road and said to Tiara, "Girl if you ever do that again, I promise to beat the living daylight out of you!"

Needless to say, we made it safely to Mount Olive, NC. I never got sleepy again! Amen! We still laugh about that today!

Chapter Seven

IN THE BIBLE

According to scripture, the wise men drove a Honda. Proof: the Bible says they were all on one Accord.

Hebrews: This book states that only the man should make the coffee... He-brews.

Homer and Gomez represent the love Yahhavah has for his adulterous children with Homer being Yahhavah and Gomez being his estranged wife.

"Get your Ruth and not your Ruth-Less", shows that there are special women out there that Yahhavah or Yahweh has chosen for you but you have to let Him lead you to the right woman.

"Wait on your Boaz and stop fooling with Bozos", is the right approach because if you choose wrong he might beat Yo-azz!

Samson and the foxes tails shows you the power of Yahhavah over his enemies.

"Plowing with Samson's Heifer", has to do with letting the enemy into the bed of your chosen one, and allowing them to steal your "pillow talk"!

"Gomez a Strumpet"... you might call her a "ho" but Yahhavah uses this illustration to show us that we should never give up on our loved ones.

Chapter Eight

STAY IN THE CHURCH

You are Now a FISH!

A Protestant moved into an all Catholic neighborhood. On Fridays he would take out his grill and cook steaks. The aroma permeated the neighborhood. Finally, a group of concerned neighbors decided that they would do something about his disruptive behavior.

They went to the Protestant neighbor and convinced him to take up Catholicism. At his catechism, the priest performed the following:

You were born a Protestant,

You were raised a Protestant,

You are now a Catholic!

Believing that the group had done the trick, they waited with baited breath for the next Friday. You see, Catholics cook fish on Fridays.

Low and behold, the next Friday, once again the delicious aroma of grilling steaks permeated the entire neighbor. The concerned citizens got together to approach the new convert but as they got close to his house they heard:

You were born a steer,

You were raised a steer,

You are now a fish!

Pick Two Hymns.

The Pastor arose and he turned to the Director of Music who had come out of the closet recently. As he opened the church services he instructed the Director of Music to choose, two hymns!

Excited that the Pastor had called him out, the Director of Music looked over the audience and near the rear of the church said "I choose him and the gentleman two seats in front of him, I choose him too!

Winning the Lottery

A special member of the church wanted to win the lottery so that she could increase her giving and tithes. Every night, she prayed to God for deliverance. She told God what she would do with the lottery. She was patient, but after several years, she got desperate.

Finally, in desperation she prostrated herself on the floor and cried out to God that she be allowed to win the lottery. She prayed, "God please do me a favor and help me win the lottery!" A booming voice came out of the clouds and said "Please do me a favor and at least buy a ticket!"

Sic Him Jesus!

An accomplished cat burglar cased a house and decided that no one was home. His usual was to search each room without the distraction of turning on the lights. As he approached the master bedroom, he heard a voice that said "Beware of Jesus!" As he looked around he spotted some beaded eyes about high and another pair near the floor.

Knowing that no one was home, he decided to turn on the lights to see who was talking. He turned on the light and there was a parrot siding in the cage and a two hundred pound Doberman sitting on the floor.

He relaxes and says "You're just a bird!" Then the parrot says, "Sic him Jesus!"

Men Who Died in the Service...

A mom and her son on Memorial Day were sitting in the audience. The little one now bored to tears, asked his mom what they were doing there. The mom attempts to explain to her curious son that this service was to honor those who died in the service. After some musing, he chimed in again and asked "Was it the 8AM or 10AM Service?"

Chapter Nine

ONE LINERS WITH A POINT

"Just color me green and call me a pickle." (Tiara Martin)

I'm trying to make chicken soup out of chicken poop!

The commission follows the mission!

A setback is just a set up for a come back! Les Brown (Ms. Mamie Brown's baby boy!)

Money don't buy happiness, neither does poverty.

If a tree falls in the woods and no one is around, does it make a sound?

Romance, without finance is a nuisance....no chance.

Don't piss in my face and tell me that it is raining. (Luby Martin)

You can ask God for Humility but... you can't thank Yahhavah for this sincere blessing. (Luby Martin)

Don't ever write a check with your mouth that your azz can't cash. (Harold Lee Martin)

I haven't seen him in a COON's age. (A coon typically lives for sixty to sixty-five years. So this refers to an elderly black man, not the raccoon in nature!)

I spent a week there ONE night! (Just pick a town, Padduca, Kentucky)

Throw them under the bus, back up and run over them again (this is passing the buck more than once)!

Don't look back while running or you will stumble forward.

No good deed goes unpunished!

That is as slick as greased snot on a door knob covered in Virgin Olive Oil.

If I had known being a Senior Citizen has such perks, I would have joined AARP a long time ago!

WELL: a deep subject

Words alone may often fail so demonstrate to make that sale.

I am trying to put a round peg in a square hole.

I am pressed for time... Like a Mummy!

My mama wanted me to be a Doctor so that everyday I could discharge patience or release patients...

I am not a Doctor because I have no patients.

Once on the lips, forever on the hips.

Facts tell, stories sell.

Just call me on time for supper.

Your Actions...Express Yourself!

"It's not what you look like, when you are doing what you're doing. It's what you are doing, when you are doing, what it looks like you are doing!"

My Money (revised)

My Money is Funny,
My Change is Strange,
My Nickel is Fickle,
My Dime lost in Time,
My Quarter like Water,
My Fifty Cents don't make Sense,
My Dollar Bill has no Thrill.
My $$$$$ is Hilarious and laughing out loud!

Becoming a Bishop...

My story. I have never been ordained as a Bishop. I have been ordained as Evangelist, Minister, Reverend, and Elder. My journey from Maryland to Florida as a Medical Missionary was often convoluted with misrepresentation of my title.

Elder was often believed to be a glorified deacon. I dropped the Reverend because Holy and Reverend is His name. I accidentally stumbled on to Bishop because in Atlanta, GA everybody is a Bishop.

So I decided that as an independent ministry, working with so many different denominations, that I could announce myself as a Bishop. When on the job in Virginia, I was paid $500 for a presentation to 300 Pastors, Deacons, Superintendents and Bible teachers.

On the way back to Georgia, I was totally blown away when I saw my honorarium! I decided that being a Bishop really pays well. I never went back to Elder again!

Chapter Ten

WHATEVER AND RISQUÉ

Drowning in Her Own Tea Pee

Any time tea is being served...

Ask if they've heard about the Native American (Indian) that drank 13 quarts of tea?

Answer: She drowned in her own TeePee!

Play on Words

Three networkers were having dinner together. They were also brothers who tried to outdo one another.

The oldest brother, an Avon salesperson says to his wife, "Pass the sugar..Sugar!"

The second eldest brother, an Atomy salesman, says to his wife, "Pass the honey...Honey!"

The youngest of the three, working with Amway, glances sort of sideways to his wife and sort of under his breath says, "Pass the tea...BAG!"

Or Would You Rather Have a Car?

The Indians (Native Americans) were being moved to a new location. One brave soul by the name of Bowels refused to leave.

When the officials went to his tent, he vehemently replied, "Bowels no move!" They called for the doctor and gave him a laxative.

The next day they approached his tent again and he shouted in defiance, "Bowels still no move!" They doubled the laxative and waited three days!

On the third day when they approached his tent, the foul odor greeted them with an unpleasant roasting aroma. Bowels opens the tent and says, "Bowels gotta move now! Teepee full of Sh!tt!"

You Can Expect...

I learned at an IBM Administrative Class
That you can always expect,
what you inspect.
After some musing I added:
And you can respect
what you detect!

What Kind of Bird Can't Fly?

This was told to my dad when he was falsely arrested!

It was not funny then, and not funny now...

Answer: A Jail Bird!

What Can A Bird Do That A Man Can Not?

Fly....A man can get on a plane.
Build a nest...A man can build a house.
Give birth...A woman needs a man to complete the process.
Eat...Men eat all the time.

Answer: A bird can eat with his "pecker!"

Knock, Knock

(To be said as you face a female with your foreheads pushed together...)

Who's there?
Emerson.
Emerson Who?
Them are some fine boobs you got there!

My Wife's Duty

Keep the bold b!tche$,
In the cold ditches
And the wicked witches,
In serious stitches!

Sisters of Mercy Whore House

A gentleman, new in town, spotted the above sign. Unbelievable, he thought to himself as he rather cautiously approached.

A rather elderly sister met him at the door and kindly welcomed him in. The second sister told him that the entrance fee is $200. He nervously fished that out of his pocket thinking that God must be frowning upon him. She then said to go down the hall to the second door on the right.

He entered the door and a very attractive, young, and vibrant sister was sitting on the bed. She says, "That will be $100 sir!" He quickly gives her the money! She says, "Go through that door and be prepared for the thrill of your life!"

He hears the door lock behind him and realizes he is now in an alley outside the convent facing a wall with a sign that reads... "Congratulations! You have just been screwed by the Sisters of Mercy!"

Favorite Exercise

I get most of my exercise jumping to conclusions.

My favorite exercise is to fill the tub with water, pull the plug, then fight the current!

One active baseball player says that when exercise or the thought of exercise comes, he then lies down until the urge passes!

Yo Mama...

Yo mama is...so fat that when she farted, you were born!

Yo mama so ugly even Rice Krispies won't talk to her!

Yo mama so ugly, she looks like she's been bobbing for apples in hot grease.

Yo momma's teeth are so yellow, when she smiled at traffic, it slowed down.

Yo momma's so fat, she brought a spoon to the Super Bowl.

Yo momma's so stupid, she put lipstick on her forehead to make up her mind.

Yo momma's so fat, when she went to the beach, all the whales started singing "We Are Family."

Yo momma's so dumb, when she went to the movies and saw the "Under 17 not permitted" sign, she left to get 16 of her friends.

Chapter Eleven

SINGING

My singing is so bad that I can't carry a note in a bucket!

Sometimes when I sing people ask if I will just sing "Nearer My God to thee", when I get to heaven.

I sing tenor and am often requested to sing "Ten or Twelve miles south of here!"

Favorite Request

Singing by request: My favorite is, "Could you please sing 'Down by the River and Far Far Away'?"

Some Closing Favorites...

Invictus

William Ernest Henley - 1849-1903

Out of the night that covers me,
Black as the Pit from pole to pole,
I thank whatever gods may be
For my unconquerable soul.

In the fell clutch of circumstance
I have not winced nor cried aloud.
Under the bludgeonings of chance
My head is bloody, but unbowed.

Beyond this place of wrath and tears
Looms but the Horror of the shade,
And yet the menace of the years
Finds, and shall find, me unafraid.

It matters not how strait the gate,
How charged with punishments the scroll,
I am the master of my fate:
I am the captain of my soul.

The Gettysburg Address

"Four score and seven years ago our fathers brought forth on this continent, a new nation, conceived in Liberty, and dedicated to the proposition that all men are created equal.

"Now we are engaged in a great civil war, testing whether that nation or any nation so conceived and so dedicated, can long endure. We are met on a great battle-field of that war. We have come to dedicate a portion of that field, as a final resting place for those who here gave their lives that that nation might live. It is altogether fitting and proper that we should do this.

"But, in a larger sense, we can not dedicate — we can not consecrate — we can not hallow — this ground. The brave men, living and dead, who struggled here, have consecrated it, far above our poor power to add or detract. The world will little note, nor long remember what we say here, but it can never forget what they did here. It is for us the living, rather, to be dedicated here to the unfinished work which they who fought here have thus far so nobly advanced. It is rather for us to be here dedicated to the great task remaining before us -- that from these honored dead we take increased devotion to that cause for which they gave the last full measure of devotion — that we here highly resolve that these dead shall not have died in vain — that this nation, under God, shall have a new birth of freedom — and that government of the people, by the people, for the people, shall not perish from the earth."

Abraham Lincoln

November 19, 1863

Amazing Grace

Amazing Grace how sweet the sound
that saved a wretch like me.
I once was lost but now I'm found,
was blind but now I see!

Twas grace that taught my heart to fear,
And grace my fears relieved.
How precious did that grace appear
The hour I first believed.

Through many dangers, toils and snares
I have already come,
'Tis grace has brought me safe thus far
And grace will lead me home.

The Lord has promised good to me
His word my hope secures;
He will my shield and portion be,
As long as life endures.

When we've been there ten thousand years
Bright shining as the sun.
We have no less days to sing God's praise,
Than when we first begun!

Lift Every Voice and Sing

James Weldon Johnson, J. Rosamond Johnson

Lift ev'ry voice and sing
'Til earth and heaven ring
Ring with the harmonies of Liberty
Let our rejoicing rise
High as the list'ning skies
Let it resound loud as the rolling sea
Sing a song full of the faith that the dark past has taught us
Sing a song full of the hope that the present has brought us

Facing the rising sun of our new day begun
Let us march on 'til victory is won
Stony the road we trod
Bitter the chastening rod
Felt in the days when hope unborn had died
Yet with a steady beat
Have not our weary feet
Come to the place for which our fathers sighed?

We have come over a way that with tears has been watered
We have come, treading our path through the blood of the slaughtered
Out from the gloomy past
'Til now we stand at last
Where the white gleam of our bright star is cast.

God of our weary years.
God of our silent tears.
Thou who has brought us thus far on the way.
Thou who has by Thy might
Led us into the light.
Keep us forever in the path, we pray.
Lest our feet stray from the places, our God, where we met Thee.
Lest, our hearts drunk with the wine of the world, we forget Thee.
Shadowed beneath Thy hand
May we forever stand.
True to our God,
True to our native land.

Epilogue

It has been a plumb,
Pleasing,
Pleasure.
As well a professional,
Private,
Personal,
Privilege,
Performing,
This programmed
Presentation
In your presence.
Thanks for participating
Patiently,
Pleasantly,
And quietly.

Mike drop!

THE END

www.ingramcontent.com/pod-product-compliance
Lightning Source LLC
Chambersburg PA
CBHW071422070526
44578CB00003B/664